D0494254

THE IRISH CIVIL WAR

First published in 2000 by
Mercier Press
PO Box 5 5 French Church St Cork
Tel: (021) 275040; Fax: (021) 274969; e.mail: books@mercier.ie
16 Hume Street Dublin 2
Tel: (01) 661 5299; Fax: (01) 661 8583; e.mail: books@marino.ie

Trade enquiries to CMD Distribution 55A Spruce Avenue
Stillorgan Industrial Park Blackrock County Dublin
Tel: (01) 294 2556; Fax: (01) 294 2564
e.mail: cmd@columba.ie

© Edward Purdon 2000
A CIP record for this book is available from the British Library.

ISBN 1 85635 300 1
10 9 8 7 6 5 4 3 2 1

This book is sold subject to the condition that it shall not, by way
of trade or otherwise, be lent, resold, hired out or otherwise
circulated without the publisher's prior consent in any form of
binding or cover other than that in which it is published and
without a similar condition being imposed on the subsequent
purchaser.

Cover photograph courtesy of the Central Catholic Library
Cover design by Penhouse Design
Printed in Ireland by ColourBooks Baldoyle Dublin 13

THE IRISH CIVIL WAR 1922–23

EDWARD PURDON

MERCIER PRESS

CONTENTS

CHRONOLOGY

1921

9 July	Truce brings to an end hostilities in Anglo-Irish War
14–21 July	Lloyd George and de Valera hold exploratory meetings in London
6 December	'Plenipotentiary' delegation led by Griffith and Collins signs Treaty
14 December	Dáil Éireann meets in UCD to debate the terms of the Treaty
15 December	De Valera's Document No. 2 offered to Dáil
19 December	Griffith introduces motion to accept Treaty terms; de Valera withdraws Document No. 2

1922

7 January	Dáil approves Griffith's motion (64–57)
9 January	De Valera resigns presidency
11 January	De Valera defeated in re-election for presidency (60–58) and Griffith elected; de Valera and supporters walk out
1 February	Pro-Treaty forces occupy Beggars Bush barracks
11 March	Irregulars cede control of Limerick to pro-Treaty troops
26 March	Banned Army Convention held in Mansion House

13 April	Irregulars occupy Four Courts, Kilmainham and buildings on the east side of O'Connell Street
20 May	Election pact announced by Collins and de Valera
14 June	Collins withdraws from pact under British pressure
16 June	General election, with greatly increased support for the Treaty
22 June	Shooting of Sir Henry Wilson in London
26 June	Kidnapping of General J. J. O'Connell, assistant chief of staff of pro-Treaty forces
28 June	Bombardment of Four Courts, marking the formal start of the Civil War
5 July	Irregular forces are defeated in O'Connell Street
12 August	Death of Arthur Griffith; William Cosgrave replaces him as head of the Provisional Government
22 August	Death of Michael Collins in an ambush in County Cork
10 October	Army Council proclamation indicating Special Emergency Powers granted by the Dáil
22 October	Irish hierarchy issues solemn pastoral letter against the Irregulars
17 November	First government executions under Special Powers (by 2 May 1923 seventy-seven republicans have been executed)
24 November	Erskine Childers shot by firing-squad while awaiting decision on appeal

30 November	Liam Lynch issues order that any TDs who voted for Special Powers measure are to be shot on sight
6 December	Irish Free State (Saorstát Éireann) comes into existence with Tim Healy as governor-general
7 December	Sean Hales TD shot dead by Irregular gunmen
8 December	Rory O'Connor, Liam Mellows and two other republican prisoners shot in Mountjoy in reprisal

1923

8 January	Eight Free State soldiers executed for 'treachery'
29 January	Liam Deasy signs instrument of 'unconditional surrender'
1 February	Army Council takes even more draconian powers, extending the death penalty to the possession of subversive papers
7 March	Eight republican prisoners blown up by landmine at Ballyseedy Cross, County Kerry
24 March	At secret meeting in County Waterford de Valera's peace proposals defeated by six votes to five, largely at the instigation of Liam Lynch; four republican prisoners executed at Drumboe, near Stranorlar, County Donegal
10 April	Liam Lynch mortally wounded in Knockmealdown mountains
30 April	Frank Aiken, new chief of staff, declares a unilateral ceasefire

9

| 24 May | Aiken orders Irregulars in the field to dump arms; de Valera issues his 'Legion of the Rearguard' proclamation |

1924

| July | Most Irregular internees, including de Valera, freed |
| 8 November | General amnesty |

1925

| 7 October | Sir James Craig repudiates in advance Boundary Commission's findings |
| 3 December | Craig, Baldwin and Cosgrave sign the tripartite agreement that determines the border between Northern Ireland and the Free State |

1

THE TREATY –
AND DOCUMENT NO. 2

The truce which called a stop to open hostilities
in the Anglo-Irish War and prepared the way
for the negotiation of the treaty which set up the
Irish Free State came into effect on 9 July 1921.
The war – really a series of localised guerrilla
raids, ambushes and brutal reprisals by the
Black and Tans and the Auxiliaries – had resulted
in the deaths of 405 RIC officers (many of them
Catholic), 150 military personnel and an esti-
mated 750 IRA members and civilians. Its
causes were both proximate and remote, coming
as it did at the end of nearly a decade of crowded
political and armed activity, but unquestionably
it began because of the end of confidence in
Redmondite constitutionalism and the successes
of Sinn Féin in the election of 1918, when in

a 48 per cent poll they won 73 out of 105 Irish seats.

John Redmond (1856–1918), Parnell's political heir, had managed to unite the Irish party sufficiently again to hold the political balance in the House of Commons in 1912 and to persuade Asquith (1852–1928) to introduce a Home Rule bill. Like his master, and earlier Daniel O'Connell, Redmond strove to avoid an armed uprising, believing with considerable justification that any such resort would harm Ireland more than its enemy. Like Parnell he underestimated the strength of Ulster Protestants' legitimate fears and the strength of their will to resist Rome Rule. The Ulster Volunteer Force (UVF), founded in 1913 to coordinate paramilitary resistance among Northern unionists, was secretly aided by elements in the Conservative party and supported by retired officers of the British army. No attempt was made to prevent the distribution of arms after the Larne gun-running of April 1914, and the Curragh mutiny (March 1914) indicated clearly to the British government that it could not count upon the obedience of some of the senior officers in the army, a number of whom were of Ulster extraction.

Asquith and his cabinet showed little resolve in the face of such historical threats, and the question of whether Ulster would resort to 'the supreme arbitrament of arms' – in the characteristic phrase of Edward Carson (1854–1935) – was about to be answered when the declaration of war on 4 August 1914 postponed, with Redmond's agreement, any decision about Home Rule. His policy of 'good behaviour', as opposed to Ulster intransigence, was continually betrayed by Britain, and his encouragement of recruiting which would, he believed, leave him after a short war with a trained army that could enforce the terms of the Home Rule legislation meant that many Irishmen, including his brother, died in the trenches of the First World War.

There were other elements in the political situation that were to be highly significant. On 1 November 1913, Professor Eoin MacNeill, one of the founders of the Gaelic League, had responded to the UVF gun-running by writing an article in the League's journal *An Claideamh Soluis* called 'The North Began' which recommended that the Home Rulers, like the UVF, should arm themselves. He was responsible for the founding of the Irish Volunteers three weeks later. Already, too, the rekindled phoenix flame fanned by John Devoy (1842–1928), the head of the American Fenian offshoot, Clan na Gael, had burst into a small but steady fire and as the regenerated Irish Republican Brotherhood (IRB) had become the incandescent element of the Volunteers. The third important force which had been generated by the Dublin lockout of 1913 was the Citizen Army of the labour leader James Connolly (1868–1916).

The 1916 Rising, in which members of these groups took part, was at first greeted by rage and derision but the dignity of the participants and the deliberately paced executions of its leaders by General Maxwell (1859–1929) resulted in a wave of support for Arthur Griffith's Sinn Féin. Many of the Volunteers, released from prison as a result of a mitigation of Maxwell's absolutism and the pressure of world opinion, constituted themselves as the Irish Republican Army (IRA) – an indication of their aim – and their numbers were swollen by young volunteers and returned, seasoned soldiers. Though nominally under the control of Sinn Féin, the various IRA forces had a great deal of local autonomy and one of the reasons for the drift into hostilities against the British was the lack of central control. The first shots of the War of Independence, in the ambush by Dan Breen and Sean Treacy (1895–1920) at Soloheadbeg, County Tipperary, on 21 January 1919, was such a local (and not formally unauthorised) operation.

The spirit of the times held life cheap; 10 million had died in the First World War and the quasi-religious fervour of 1916 still fired the more extreme republicans, notably Michael Collins, who was an effective general of operations. Many young men, imbued with exalted patriotism and having a role to play for the first time in their mundane lives, welcomed the call to arms. Pure, self-regarding republicanism, in which no sacrifice of self or others was too great for the cause, was by definition tunnel-visioned, and it left the participants with no urge to negotiate and ill-equipped to do so should the need arise. De Valera, who had feared and loathed violence since his days as a successful Easter Week commander, knew that a war was almost inevitable in the circumstances but did his best to avert it, knowing that some kind of negotiated settlement was inevitable. The attitude of the British government – the coalition that was led by Lloyd George from 1916 but was heavily dependent on the support of the extreme unionist, the Canadian Bonar Law – was notably unhelpful. The arrest of de Valera and Griffith in May 1918 on the fictitious charge that they were involved in a German plot left Collins and Cathal Brugha free to prepare for a chosen armed confrontation.

One less-noticed result of the Rising was that Lloyd George decided in June 1916 to partition the country, giving Home Rule to most of Ireland but excluding the 'Protestant' north-east. Redmond did what he could to fight the proposal and succeeded in cutting the counties of exclusion from the nine counties of historical Ulster to the six that presently constitute Northern Ireland, while accepting Lloyd George's assurance that the exclusion would be temporary. When in 1920 the IRA were engaged in their war essentially against the Home Rule proposals originally agreed by Redmond, Lloyd George passed, virtually without opposition, the Government of Ireland Act, which set up regimes in Dublin and Belfast. Sinn Féin's policy of abstention meant that there was no parliamentary debate and no possibility of mitigation of the measure, which left the Ulster nationalists (a third of the population) permanently under unionist governments which were to last until 18 July 1973, when the Belfast parliament was abolished. Just as during the Treaty negotiations, minds were concentrated on other topics.

The invitation to treat was to expose in the republican side considerable divisions, which had been ignored during the fighting. The delegation had against them the Welsh wizard Lloyd George, the most consummate and capable politician of the age, and he was backed by

Churchill, the most charismatic leader of the next generation. The negotiations, over which hung the threat of a British ultimatum (finally pronounced by Lloyd George as 'war within three days' on 6 December 1921), were long and tortuous in the extreme; Lord Longford's magisterial book on the subject, *Peace by Ordeal* (1935), was well named. There were two unexpected features of the team of delegates: the presence of Michael Collins and the absence of de Valera. Collins probably accepted his role out of duty, although his name was as strongly associated with hardline militarism as were those of Cathal Brugha (who refused to go to London), Austin Stack, Oscar Traynor and Rory O'Connor (who did not even approve the truce). His presence there was intended as an assurance that any agreement by him would be accepted by the IRA.

De Valera's motives for remaining in Dublin are still uncertain. Critics say that he resented the growth of Collins's personal standing, which had surprised him on his return from his fundraising tour of the United States (1 June 1919– 23 December 1920). They say, too, that he knew from earlier discussions with Lloyd George that the likely outcome of the negotiations would be a compromise unacceptable to many republicans and he did not wish to be associated with that 'betrayal'. This view is almost certainly unjust and too simplistic, considering the subtle, not to say machiavellian, nature of the president's mind. (It also ignores the sense of moral scruple that he believed permeated his whole existence.) He was busy working on an 'external association' arrangement that was eventually called Document No. 2 and which he thought would have been more palatable to the ultras in the vexed question of the remaining connection with Britain and the oath of allegiance. He was regarded (and regarded himself) as a kind of head of state and as such should not, he felt, be engaged in the minutiae of negotiation any more than George V. He hoped, too, that in the event of open and armed hostility to Treaty terms, he would have a sufficiently impartial air to prevent extreme violence.

The team were regarded (certainly by the British) as 'plenipotentiaries' who had the power to make final decisions, but this was later disputed. The important question of Ulster, which should have been the clause on which negotiations broke down, went by default; as before, in the debate on the Government of Ireland Act, the Southern nationalists allowed themselves to be distracted. They settled for Lloyd George's offer of a boundary commission, which they believed would deliver counties Tyrone and Fermanagh, Derry city and Newry into the new Free State. They knew that this would still leave many nationalists under a government which would regard them with suspicion and which would use most of its energies to prevent them having access to political power, but they could not take seriously the idea that Northern Ireland might have other than a very temporary existence. Collins was already considering a policy of non-cooperation with the new state; he intended this policy to become more aggressive as time went on.

In fact the fate of the North was not of immediate concern to the more vociferous republican anti-Treatyites; what they wanted was a republic and a complete break with the king and Commonwealth. The document that Griffith and Collins signed limited Irish independence in several ways: the Irish Free State would have the same status within the empire as Canada; there would be a governor-general, the king's representative; the Royal Navy and the RAF would have rights of operation in certain Irish ports; and the members of the Dáil would have to swear allegiance (in the first instance) to the constitution of the Irish Free State and then to the king and his successors 'in virtue of the common citizenship of Ireland with Great Britain' and her membership of the British Commonwealth of Nations. The order of swearing was regarded as significant but in the end did not signify; those who accepted the terms shrugged their shoulders and followed the form; nothing on earth would have moved the ultras even to recognise the 'Crown' let alone swear allegiance to it. The irrelevant Crown had the same iconic power for the British as the idea of a free, independent Irish republic had for the IRA, but its imposition as a condition on republicans was notably un-helpful in the circumstances.

Document No. 2, de Valera's alternative, would have placed all authority with the Irish people but would have bound them in an association with other members of the existing Commonwealth, recognising the king as president of the association. Significantly, there was no oath of greater allegiance than befitted the recognition of the king as head of the Commonwealth. Of equal importance was the temporary acquiescence in the Treaty terms with regard to Northern Ireland. De Valera had hoped that this compromise would satisfy the more extreme republicans but they would not – and psychologically could not – settle for anything less than a free republic. It was what Pearse had died for, and the spirit of Easter Week was still alive. In the circumstances, ingenious as Document No. 2 was, it was not acceptable to any on the British side either. Indeed the terms of the Treaty as accepted by the plenipotentiaries appalled the Conservatives, Bonar Law claiming that these terms left Sinn Féin the option of in time declaring the republic that it sought. In this he unwittingly anticipated Collins's description of the agreement in Dáil Éireann on 19 December, thirteen days after the signing, as 'the freedom to obtain freedom'.

2

THE FOUR COURTS

The Treaty terms were vigorously debated in the Dáil on twelve days between 14 December and 7 January – the Christmas recess lasting from 22 December until 3 January. The debates took place in the council chamber of UCD in Earlsfort Terrace because the Mansion House in Dawson Street, where the first Dáil had met, was occupied by a Christmas fête. Many of the TDs were IRA commanders who had been returned unopposed in the 1920 election. Though the candidates had a considerable following there was undoubtedly a certain amount of local intimidation. The 1918 Dáil had been elected on a minority vote and there is some justice in the assertion that the personalities who were now settling Ireland's future were just about representative of the country's wishes. On Thursday 15 December de Valera proposed his own document, withdrawing it again on the nineteenth when Griffith introduced the motion, seconded by Seán Mac Eoin, 'that Dáil Éireann approves the Treaty between Great Britain and Ireland signed in London on December 6th, 1921'. He had discovered by then that the population at large was strongly in favour of the terms. A majority of the plain people of Ireland were anxious to accept what seemed to them very good terms, unaware that they agreed instinctively with Collins when he wrote in a letter to a friend on the day the Treaty was signed: 'Think – what I have got for Ireland! Something which she has wanted these past seven hundred years.' (The letter continued with ominous accuracy: 'Will anyone be satisfied at the bargain? Will anyone? I tell you this – early this morning I signed my death warrant.')

De Valera's incessant but carefully modulated contributions were in noted contrast to the exalted and fiery speeches of the other anti-Treaty members. Only once during the night-marish drift towards civil war did he engage in apocalyptic republican rhetoric: on St Patrick's Day at Thurles in an almost hysterical speech he spoke of the need the IRA might have to 'wade through Irish blood, through the blood of the soldiers of the Irish government and through, perhaps, the blood of some of the members of the government in order to get Irish freedom'. Supporters say the speech was meant as a warning; critics, with more justice, condemn it as incitement; as prophecy it proved to be only too precise.

Most of the anti-Treatyites spoke of betrayal – the more extreme members unmoved by the pragmatic logic of Griffith and rejecting Collins's interpretation of the agreement's potential. They had elevated the cause of Ireland's republican freedom to the level almost of religious belief. No mere considerations of the possible were to be allowed to leaven the purity of the ideals of the 1916 Proclamation. The exaltation of battle was no preparation for the fustian business of democracy and in the heat of the verbal rancour the opposition did not seem to realise that the Treatyites shared their sense of disappointment. Most had no concept of the tedium of much parliamentary business and, as the reports of proceedings show, parliamentary language had not been learned. Old comrades found themselves on opposing sides and personal animosities that had been papered over during the war now showed as gaping cracks. Cathal Brugha in a characteristically intemperate outburst decried Collins's contribution to the success of the struggle, claiming that he was a mere publicity-seeker, a creation of the newspapers. Erskine Childers, who had acted as secretary to the delegation but had not signed the Treaty, revealed himself as one of the agreement's coldest and most bitter opponents. He was joined in extreme rhetoric by the women of the Dáil, including Pearse's mother, Terence MacSwiney's sister, Tom Clarke's widow and the Countess Markievicz – which caused the group to be known, with the inevitable splash of black Irish humour, as the 'women and Childers party'.

The Dáil approved the Treaty on 7 January 1922 but by a very close margin: sixty-four to fifty-seven. Two days later de Valera resigned the presidency of the Dáil and when on 10

January he was rejected on a motion of re-election by sixty votes to fifty-eight he walked out of the room, followed by the rest of the 'antis'. Tempers were high: Collins shouted 'Deserters all!' to be answered by cries of 'Up the Republic!' and when Con Markievicz called the remaining deputies oath-breakers and cowards, Collins roared 'Foreigners! Americans! English!' – a not-too-subtle reference to the presumed nationalities of the countess, de Valera and Childers. It was clear that most of the IRA commanders – such as Rory O'Connor, director of engineering during the war; Cathal Brugha, IRA chief of staff; Austin Stack, deputy chief of staff; Liam Mellows; Liam Lynch; and Ernie O'Malley – and many others would accept neither the terms of the Treaty nor the nature and personnel of the Provisional Government that was about to be set up as the British authorities began the handover of power. Personal psychology was as significant a determinant of decision as record of active service and idealism. There were no more grimly dedicated activists in the war than Collins, Richard Mulcahy and Seán

Mac Eoin; yet they were prepared to accept the terms and work within them eventually to improve them. Another factor, impossible fully to interpret, was the fact that most of the dramatis personae were under forty. Only Arthur Griffith, who was to die the following August at the age of fifty-one, was the more likely age for a statesman.

The fissure grew wider, causing a sociological and psychological split in the country and providing a hateful means of personal identification for nearly three generations of Irish people who should have been looking eagerly forwards rather than meanly backwards. Even now the rancour of the time can surface in unlikely and petty controversies. The response of the 'antis' was instinctively militaristic. Power, in the shape of arms, rested with the largely anti-Treaty IRA. Collins and Mulcahy worked as swiftly as they could to build up a legitimate national force that would be the arm of the provisional government that slowly edged out of the Dáil. Rory O'Connor, who had emerged as the chief spokesman for those who were soon to be called the 'Irregulars', demanded a convention of what Mulcahy still referred to as the 'army of the Republic'. The latter temporised, finding excellent reasons for postponing what promised to be an incendiary gathering.

Meanwhile the handover of power was going more smoothly than anyone had expected. A significant moment was the 'surrender' of Dublin Castle to Collins by Lord Fitzalan, the Viceroy. One probably true anecdote from the event states that he chided Collins for being seven minutes late and Collins replied, 'We've been waiting seven hundred years; you can have the seven minutes.' The British army's strength was steadily diminished until by May 1922 only the Dublin garrison of 5,000 men remained, and by the time the demobilisation of the RIC began, at the end of March, all the Black and Tans and Auxiliaries had gone away to cover themselves with further glory. Not all approved of the ending of the army connection; in garrison towns like Athlone and Fermoy the soldiers' commissariat contracts and individual buying power were sorely missed. And the departure of the RIC, on the whole a respected force, left the country effectively without any formal system of maintenance of public order outside Dublin, where the lofty members of the Dublin Metropolitan Police still patrolled the streets.

This hiatus began to be filled on 21 February with the establishment of the Civic Guard, whose members at the start of their careers had side arms but no uniforms. The force was intended to replicate the RIC but unrest among the members led to a mutiny in August. Eoin O'Duffy, who had been assistant chief of staff of the IRA, working under instruction from Kevin O'Higgins, was given the task of reconstruction, and the body he produced, the Garda Síochána, an unarmed consensual force established on 8 August 1923, quickly gained public support. The Civic Guard figured in the ultimatum issued by the Irregulars under O'Connor and Mellows after they occupied the Four Courts and other city-centre buildings on 13 April. They wanted its disbandment and refused to recognise the Provisional Government, which was determined to maintain the army as the IRA. They would not countenance the holding of any election 'while the threat of war by England exists'.

The choice of the Four Courts (and the buildings on the east side of O'Connell Street) was symbolic rather than tactical, much as that of the GPO had been exactly six years earlier. As ever, symbols took precedence over practicalities; the destruction of the Law Library and the Public Record Office, with priceless archive records of a thousand years of Irish history, was motivated by the same nihilism. Flickering flames of Irregular activity had already been noted around the country, and Mulcahy's armed forces did what they could do quench them. Irregulars had some successful seizures of arms at Helvic Head in Waterford and Cobh harbour. The occupation of Beggars Bush barracks on 1 February by pro-Treaty forces (sent in at 4 am) prevented the Irregulars from seizing it, and an internal coup planned for the eve of the Volunteer Convention of 26 March was forestalled. The Civil War, as a whole, was fought by forces not entirely loyal on either side. Many of the prison guards in Mountjoy were sympathetic to the Irregular prisoners and there was no operational split in the IRA in the North, since both factions were active in doing what they could to defend Ulster Catholics against essentially government-approved pogroms. Collins and Mulcahy found themselves in the anomalous position of supplying arms to Irregulars in Belfast and Derry. The situation there, though forecast precisely by Northern nationalists, seemed, as did most things in Ulster, to surprise Dublin. One of the direr aspects of the internecine struggle in the South was that it distracted Collins's attention from the crisis in Ulster.

The first indication of a serious threat of civil war was the Army Convention, held in in the Mansion House on 26 March 1922, in spite of the fact that it had been prohibited by Mulcahy. The 220 anti-Treaty delegates from forty-nine brigades were still smarting from the occupation of Limerick by pro-Treaty forces – urban fighting prevented only by the personal intervention of Oscar Traynor and Liam Lynch. After the convention its spokesman Rory O'Connor repudiated the authority of Dáil Éireann, clearly expecting that any election would reaffirm commitment to the Treaty terms. O'Connor was asked if he agreed that the logical inference of his ultimatum was a military dictatorship; his reply was typical of the man and the movement: 'You can take it that way if you like.' (In time O'Connor would repudiate even the anti-Treaty council, when they refused him permission to attack the remaining British forces in Ireland.) The first victims of the now openly militant Irregulars were the presses of the pro-Treaty *Freeman's Journal* (1763–1924), which had not reported the convention to their satisfaction.

Still anxious to prevent greater hostilities, Collins and de Valera worked during May on a pact that would essentially rig the results of the general election that was due to create the third Dáil. (De Valera did not necessarily believe in democratic principles at the time: he was at his most pedagogical – or even episcopal – when he stated that 'the majority have not the right to do wrong'. His remarkable conscience was able to ignore the statement by the Catholic hierarchy on 26 April that they considered that 'the best and wisest course is for Ireland to accept the Treaty and make the most of the freedom that it undoubtedly brings'.) By the terms of the pact all nationalist candidates would stand as Sinn Féin, unopposed and in proportion to the seats they held in the second Dáil. The pact caused uproar in Westminster and resulted in the same kind of anti-Catholic activity in the North that had followed the occupation of the Four Courts. The Treaty visibly trembled, with threats from London of closing the border and of occupying Dublin. Collins and Griffith again yielded to the threat of a new British onslaught. In the election which followed on 16 June the anti-Treatyites were decisively defeated and the results showed the beginnings of more normal politics: Pro-Treaty, 58; Anti-Treaty 36; Labour, 17; Farmers, 7; Independents, 6; TCD, 6.

Before the full significance of these results could be analysed the assassination of Field Marshal Sir Henry Wilson on 22 June by two IRA members, Reginald Dunne and Joseph O'Sullivan, who were hanged on 10 August, caused a further crisis. Wilson had figured largely in the Curragh incident and as security adviser to the Northern Ireland government was held responsible for the Ulster pogroms. (The day after his death three Catholic youths were shot in cold blood by B-specials in Cushendall, County Antrim.) It is likely that Collins knew and approved of the killing. It precipitated the formal opening of the war, which is dated from the pro-Treaty attack on the Four Courts at 4 am on 28 June. Lloyd George had written immediately to Collins, demanding that he take action against the Dublin Irregulars, assuming – or choosing to assume – that it had been an Irregular operation. General Macready, the Dublin GOC, was ordered to take the courts on 24 June but wisely ignored his instructions, knowing that it would spell the end of the Treaty. As it was he provided Collins with the artillery which finally brought about the surrender. Collins still hesitated but the kidnapping of General J. J. ('Ginger') O'Connell in reprisal for the arrest of Leo Henderson, who had tried to commandeer cars to mount an attack on the North, caused him to give the order to evacuate the Four Courts and surrender the garrison.

The defenders issued a characteristic communiqué which called upon 'our former comrades of the Irish Republic to return to that allegiance and thus guard the Nation's honour from the infamous stigma that her sons aided her foes in retaining a hateful domination over her.' It also apostrophied 'the sacred spirits of the illustrious Dead' who were with them 'in this great struggle'. The taking of a 'British' institution with British shells turned on fellow Irishmen gave them another symbolic victory but it was clear that the now well-armed pro-Treaty forces, who had the option of using British soldiers, would be the inevitable victors. Though outnumbered 'down the country' in the ratio 4:1, they soon secured Dublin. The city conflict left 65 dead and 281 seriously wounded, the most notable casualty being Cathal Brugha, who rushed out into Talbot Street from the back of his headquarters in the Granville Hotel, shooting at the lines of pro-Treaty troops. He died two days later. The members of the

Four Courts garrison, including O'Connor and Mellows, were interned in Mountjoy. On 8 August Cork was taken by sea and by the end of that month, one of the most tragic in Ireland's history, the Civil War had become a grisly copy of the opportunistic raid-and-ambush pattern of the Anglo-Irish War.

3

EMERGENCY POWERS

Worried by continuing violence in Ulster –
in which nationalist dead and severely
wounded were in the ratio of 4:1 to Protestant fatalities and which tended to break out
in response to events in the South – and
weary of the grind of politics, Collins turned
with something like relief and even his old
enthusiasm to the task of finishing the war
as quickly as possible. The horror of it
appalled him and he resented the emotional
toll of the idea of a brothers' conflict. He
was ever-anxious to find some kind of
peaceful settlement but was determined to
end hostilities by force if necessary. At the
start of the fighting the Irregulars had a
majority of trained men and arms but this
disproportion was dealt with by intensive

recruiting into the national army and a steady supply of guns and ammunition, including field artillery, from Britain. By the end of the war Britain had provided £1 million worth of arms and supplies to the Free State.

On 20 July both Waterford and Limerick were secured by government forces, the latter after vicious fighting at Kilmallock, and the IRA, now led by Liam Lynch, fell behind a line between those cities that could mark a notional eastern boundary of his 'Munster Republic'. Lynch had been captured during the fighting in Dublin but was released by Mulcahy in the belief that as an internal adversary of Rory O'Connor he would act as a kind of de-mobiliser. In fact he became an implacable pursuer of the fighting, growing more resolute with each reverse. His forces reverted to the guerrilla tactics that they had perfected during the Anglo-Irish War, but now with nothing like the support they had enjoyed then. Even then some of the 'support' resulted not from approval of the cause but out of intimidation; now Treatyites could expect little quarter. Kevin O'Higgins, one of the younger (born 1892) but most effective members of the cabinet described the Irregulars' activities as consisting of 20 per cent idealism, 20 per cent crime and 60 per cent 'sheer futility'. The pattern of robbing banks and post offices, blowing up bridges and unofficial billeting that was characteristic of the earlier struggle seemed to most of the population – even of Munster – to be pointless. Battles at Dundalk, Blessington, Clonmel, Sligo, Tuam, Tipperary and Cahir were followed by the withdrawal of anti-Treaty forces.

One of Collins's closest friends, Harry Boland, was shot by a young soldier during an arrest attempt at a hotel in Skerries on 31 July. Accounts of the incident range from the view that the incident constituted the shooting down of an unarmed man to the idea that it was a killing to prevent the escape of a known Irregular quartermaster. What actually happened is unclear but Boland had demanded to see the officer-in-charge and was moving towards the door of his bedroom when the shot that caused his death three days later was fired. Collins grieved even more at the death of his closest friend than over that of his old comrade Brugha. The terrible pain of a civil war in a small country, fought between old comrades, was becoming very clear. Collins, now commander-in-chief, was ever more anxious to end the killing and used all his capacity for undercover initiative to try to arrange to talk to Lynch and the other members of the Irregulars who were still holding out.

Fermoy, the last town held by them, was evacuated on 11 August but any satisfaction the government might have felt was dissipated by the sudden death of Griffith from a cerebral haemorrhage the next morning. He had been ill for some weeks (and was clearly weary of the bitterness and attrition that the Treaty had engendered) but insisted in carrying on cabinet business. In a sense his work was done; his foundation of Sinn Féin and insistence on the Irishness of Ireland had made a huge contribution to the national confidence and laid the intellectual and social basis for an independent country. His mien during the eight months of his presidency was appropriate for the time, consolidating the new state in spite of violent opposition to its survival and holding out for democracy against the more convenient militarism.

Collins's decision to go to Cork after Griffith's funeral was disapproved of by many of his closest advisers. He would be travelling through Irregular country and, whatever boost to morale his physical presence might engender, the risks seemed too great. His main purpose was the hope of negotiating an end to the killing, and it seemed incumbent upon him to go into 'enemy' territory, since the anti-Treatyites were in no position – and had little inclination – to come to him. Though in poor physical and mental shape and deeply depressed by the condition of the country, North and South, he insisted with forced cheerfulness that ' . . . my fellow countrymen won't kill me'. Irregular intelligence, however, knew he was going to be in his native county and the prize was irresistible. An ambush party was in position at Béal na mBláth on the Bandon–Macroom road for most of the day of

Tuesday 22 August and was on the point of breaking up when Collins's party arrived. It is generally agreed that if, as he was advised, the small convoy had driven fast along the road – blockaded only by a cart, which was quickly removed – Collins would have been safe. Instead he seized a rifle and returned fire. He was hit by a ricochet in the base of the skull and was dead by 9.30 that August evening.

The blow to the country was incalculable: Ulster nationalists had lost the one member of the Dublin government who had kept their plight perpetually before his eyes and who might have had the charisma and intelligence to secure better conditions from the unionist government; the Irregulars no longer had a friend at court – one who knew and understood the depth of their feelings and who might have prevented the atrocities on both sides that were the rule in the latter days of the struggle; the government, already bereft of Griffith's political experience and moral force, lost a vigorous, intelligent and maturing statesman; and the country lost its 'laughing boy', its folk hero, whose handsome physical presence, emphasised in his general's uniform, might in the end have won the ideal of a united, independent, peaceful Ireland. De Valera had known that Collins was in Cork and was aware of the intention to ambush him. He dreaded it for the typical reason that ' . . . he was a big man and might negotiate. If things fall into the hands of lesser men there is no telling what might happen.' He tried without success to get the local brigade to call off the ambush and after Collins's death did what he could to persuade Lynch to stop the war, with equal lack of success.

Collins's funeral in Glasnevin on 28 August attracted huge crowds but the story of his official reputation since is a miserable one. While de Valera was in power or in a position of influence he did what he could to play down Collins's reputation and significance. Successive Fianna Fáil governments did everything in their power to hinder the Collins family from erecting a suitable memorial over what was a simple military grave. De Valera personally withheld permission for a cross of Carrara marble and insisted upon a limestone

one, the total cost not to exceed £300 and the erection to be private and with no publicity. As late as 1965 a handbook entitled *Facts about Ireland*, published by the Department of Foreign Affairs, had no photograph of Collins and the following year de Valera refused to become a patron of a Michael Collins Foundation, set up by the subject's old friend Joe McGrath (1887–1966), the founder of the Irish Hospitals Trust. Insofar as history is understood or even known by later generations, Collins's name lives on as that of a hero of Irish history and is now even better known than Pearse, Parnell or O'Connell, thanks to the success of Neil Jordan's almost historical film about him. Its making was perhaps timely; the Irish are not obsessed by their history, as their detractors claim, but rather are held in the vice of imprecise prejudice.

Though many of Collins's old comrades on the anti-Treaty side were devastated by the unthinkable loss that his death represented, their more immediate concern was fear of reprisal. The numbers of those guarding Irregular prisoners had to be increased to prevent private punitive response. Mulcahy, a vigorous if less gifted man than Collins, did what he could to continue the dead general's military policies, insofar as he could interpret them. The cabinet had decided even before the third Dáil met on 9 September to appoint William Cosgrave, who had been acting chairman since Griffith's death, as president. He proved a conservative and stoical politician – a safe pair of hands who would patiently create the new Free State out of its revolutionary disarray, give it its honourable if unadventurous character and prepare it for its maturity as a nation state. The choice was deliberate since, although he had fought in 1916 (with Eamon Ceannt and Cathal Brugha in the South Dublin Union), he was a civilian and left the continuation of the war to Mulcahy, who was appointed GOC of the Provisional Government's armed forces. The separation of the two systems was deliberate, a counter to any suggestion of a military dictatorship and a deliberate contrast to the perceived intentions of O'Connor and Lynch.

The autumn of 1922 saw the beginnings of the guerrilla war west of the Shannon and south of the Suir. Connacht had been relatively quiet during the Anglo-Irish War and it was not always possible to determine whether the Civil War incidents there were part of the current struggle or a recrudescence of much older hatreds. There was some activity around Tuam in July, August and September but in general things were low-key. The province had its share of the frightfulness of reprisal execution as the bitterness of the conflict intensified during the winter and the following spring. Between 28 September and 10 October an order, largely the work of Kevin O'Higgins, was rushed through the Dáil; the order announced an amnesty for all who were willing to lay down their arms 'in the present state of armed rebellion and insurrection' but gave the Army Council special powers to try in military courts and punish anyone who was in breach of the regulations, which became law on 15 October.

The offences – which could be punished by, in ascending order, fine, internment, imprisonment, deportation, penal servitude and death – included the 'taking part in or aiding and abetting any attacks upon the National forces'; looting, arson and other damage to public or private property; and, most significantly, the possession of 'any bomb, or articles in the nature of a bomb, or any dynamite, or gelignite, or other explosive substance, or any revolver, rifle, gun or other firearm or lethal weapon, or any ammunition for such firearm'. The document was issued from General Headquarters, Portobello Barracks, on 10 October and signed on behalf of the Army Council by Risteárd Ua Maolcatha, General Commander-in-Chief. At about the same time, in what was regarded as a form of interference with the freedom of the press, special instructions were sent from government offices to editors and subs as to nomenclature in relation to the reporting of incidents in the war. The army was to be referred to as the 'national army', 'Irish army' or just 'troops'; the Irregulars were not to be described as either 'forces' or 'troops', nor were their leaders to be given their ranks; articles or letters about the treatment of Irregular prisoners were not to be published and in newspaper stories the words 'republicans', 'attacked', 'commandeered' and 'arrested' were to be replaced by 'Irregulars', 'fired at', 'seized' and 'kidnapped' respectively. Something very like the martial law that Rory O'Connor had threatened had been imposed by the other side.

A document that came from a different source but was just as compelling for some of the concerned parties was read at all Masses on Sunday 22 October. The Irish Catholic hierarchy, which had already indicated its attitude to the Treaty by its statement in April, now published a joint pastoral condemning Irregular resistance to the Provisional Government and its forces. The letter, signed by Cardinal Logue (1840–1924) and the other bishops, said that 'a section of the community' had 'wrecked Ireland from end to end', that 'a Republic without popular recognition behind it is a contradiction in terms' and that 'all those . . . who participate in such crimes are guilty of the gravest sins and may not be absolved in Confession, nor admitted to Holy Communion, if they purpose to persevere in such evil courses'. Apologists for the anti-Treaty forces have regarded this excommunication as the granting of a kind of licence to the Provisional Government to proceed with seventy-seven executions of Irregular prisoners between November and the following May. This view is rather simplistic and the reasoning behind it flawed but the Church's stance did increase the government's moral authority in its extreme response to Irregular attacks. From the perspective of seventy-five years the executions strike us as draconian, but they were perceived as necessary at the time and there were no complaints about them from the population at large.

The first well-known figure to die was Erskine Childers, who had been execrated as an 'Englishman' by the pro-Treatyites and had been an extremely effective chief of Irregular propaganda. He was arrested on 11 November and found to be in possession of a gun – a pearl-handled revolver that had been a present from Collins. This may have been a technicality but it was enough to secure the death penalty for four 'unknowns' – James Fisher, Peter Cassidy, John F. Gaffney and Richard Twohig – who were executed six days later in Kilmainham. As it was, Childers was shot (on 14 November) while awaiting the result of an appeal – a flagrant breach of his civil rights. The grief and vengeful rage at Collins's killing were still strong. These deaths were followed on 30 November by an order from Liam Lynch that all TDs who had voted for the legislation under which Childers had been executed were to be shot on sight. A week later, on 7 December, Sean Hales and the Leas-Ceann Comhairle of the Dáil, Pádraic Ó Máille, were attacked while travelling to the Dáil in an open car. Hales died and Ó Máille was seriously wounded.

The cabinet met and selected from the anti-Treatyite prisoners four representatives of the movement – Rory O'Connor (who had been Kevin O'Higgins's best man), Liam Mellows, Joe McKelvey and Richard Barrett – one from each province; they were executed the next morning in Mountjoy. This course of action was ruthless but effective since no further attacks were made on TDs but the wound inflicted by that decision festered for years and was the main cause of the death of O'Higgins's father, who was shot in his home in Stradbally, Queen's County, on 11 February 1923, and of his own death four and a half years later. On 10 December the house of Sean McGarry TD was fired while one of his children was still inside and it was said that rescue attempts were forbidden. The boy died and the verdict of the inquest was wilful murder. It was as bleak a Christmas as Ireland had experienced for many years.

In spite of the tales of killings, torture of prisoners and general frightfulness the political machine continued to operate. The Irish Free State (officially 'Saorstát Éireann') came into existence on 6 December 1922 and its first postage stamp, value 2d, showing a map of Ireland, was issued. (For other denominations British stamps, with the head of George V overprinted with 'Saorstát Éireann', continued to be used.) Tim Healy, Parnell's nemesis, was appointed governor-general-designate by George V. The Senate had its first meeting on 11 December, with Lord Glenavy (1851–1931), father of the humorist Patrick Campbell, as its chairman. It was clear that the Free State was a fact; it was becoming clearer that the Northern Ireland state, then relatively peaceful, was also a fact. Anti-Treatyism was beaten but the mopping-up would be protracted and bloody. The mindset of the Irregulars, if anything, hardened, and 'military necessity', to use Mulcahy's phrase, was used on both sides to excuse murderous brutality. Yeats's 'terrible beauty' had become a terrible ugliness.

4

LEGION OF THE REARGUARD

The 'tide of bitterness', to use de Valera's words written in an article in the American journal the *Irish Word,* continued to rise. On 8 January 1923 eight Free State soldiers were executed for treachery and there were fears of mutiny and large-scale desertions. On the same day the Army Council issued another stark order extending the power of the military courts and in a fuller statement on 1 February assumed the option of executing any person having possession of any 'plan, document or note, for a purpose prejudicial to the safety of the State or of the National forces'.

Throughout the conflict the implacability of the leaders was mitigated somewhat by the wavering of absolute allegiance on both sides but local confrontations could result in such atrocities as to suggest that scores from much older times were being settled. Seventeen Irregular prisoners were killed in the first fortnight of March in County Kerry alone. In one particularly nauseating incident at Ballyseedy on 7 March, in reprisal for the dynamiting at Knocknagoshel of five 'Staters' (one of whom had a reputation for torturing prisoners), eight men were tied to a log and blown to pieces by a mine, a ninth miraculously escaping when he was blown clear. In Cahirciveen on 12 March the same technique was used on five others, with the added refinement that they were shot in the legs first. Donegal, too, had its own incident when on 14 March four IRA men – Charlie Daly, Tim O'Sullivan, Dan Enright and Sean Larkin – were executed at Drumboe, in woods near Stranorlar. There were no unsavoury details of these killings apart from the summary nature of the executions – the automatic sentence for those found carrying arms.

Efforts to end the killings continued; Liam Deasy, who had led an IRA brigade in west Cork, was by now convinced that the prolongation of the war was pointless and actually damaging to the republican cause. He was about to make his feelings known to the Irregular executive when in mid-January he was captured by Free State soldiers and sentenced to death. While being held in Clonmel Borstal he decided to approach his captors with a plan to appeal to other commanders to surrender. Later in Arbour Hill he agreed to sign a document worded by the Free State authorities:

> I have undertaken for the future of Ireland to accept and aid in the immediate and unconditional surrender of all arms and men as required by General Mulcahy.

This declaration having been signed, he was permitted to elaborate his reasons in a longer document. It had an inevitable effect on morale and in its common sense appealed to all but the most adamant of the IRA leaders. Lynch was not convinced and called a meeting of sixteen senior commandants on 24 March in the remote Nire Valley in County Waterford. De Valera attended (although he was not allowed to take

'A fateful hour'. Artist's impression of British and Irish delegates at the Downing Street conference on the Treaty
(Illustrated London News Picture Library)

Signatures on the Treaty, including that of Michael Collins (second from top in right-hand column), who in a letter written at the time expressed his fear that, by signing the Treaty, 'I may have signed my own death warrant.'
(from the *Voice of Ireland*, courtesy Central Catholic Library)

Michael Collins at the time of the Treaty negotiations
(from the *Voice of Ireland*, courtesy Central Catholic Library)

Éamon de Valera (centre) and the four envoys to foreign countries who supported the anti-Treaty position – front row, left to right, Harry Boland, Seán T. Ó Ceallaigh, Art O'Brien and C. O'Byrne – during the Treaty Debates at the National University Buildings in Earlsfort Terrace, Dublin

Women scouts of the Republican Army – left to right, Linda Kearns, Eithne Coyle and Mae Burke – at rifle practice in Carlow shortly after their escape from Mountjoy Jail

The new National Army, in the process of taking over from the evacuating British forces
(from the *Voice of Ireland*, courtesy Central Catholic Library)

part in the significant deliberations), bringing proposals which amounted to an acceptance of the Treaty terms but with freedom granted to objectors to pursue the ultimate ideal of an independent republican state by non-violent means. Lynch could not be persuaded that the battle, if not the war, had been lost and was able to persuade others to join with him in defeating the peace proposals by six votes to five.

The war dragged on as cruelties on both sides continued. It was clear by the end of spring that the Free State forces were massing for a final solution. Then on 10 April Liam Lynch was mortally wounded in an engagement near Newcastle in his stronghold in the Knockmealdowns. Frank Aiken, who replaced him as chief of staff and who had spoken fervently for the acceptance of de Valera's proposals the previous month, was anxious now for their acceptance. He declared a unilateral ceasefire on 30 April. Cosgrave rejected any peace proposals which did not include decommissioning of arms held by the IRA and he could not by the accepted constitution permit republican TDs who had not taken the oath of allegiance to sit in the Dáil. Any continuation of the struggle was now accepted as murderous folly; on 24 May Aiken ordered anti-Treaty troops still in the field to 'dump arms'. The call to give up the struggle was accompanied by a message addressed rather operatically to the 'Soldiers of the Republic, Legion of the Rear-guard' by de Valera. It began:

> The Republic can no longer be defended successfully by your arms. Further sacrifice of life would now be vain and continuance of the struggle in arms unwise in the national interest and prejudicial to the future of our cause. Military victory must be allowed to rest with those who have destroyed the Republic. Other means must be sought to safeguard the nation's right.

He went on to reassure them that 'much that you set put to accomplish is achieved' and that the people, exhausted by seven years of intense effort, would 'rally again to the standard' and that 'when they are ready, you will be, and your place will be again as of old with the vanguard'.

As well as the seventy-seven republicans who had been executed (including six in Tuam, three in Tralee and three in Ennis as late as April and May 1923), there were 850 other casualties. The numbers imprisoned or interned had reached a total of 11,480 by 1 July; these included all the surviving Irregular commanders, among them Austin Stack and Dan Breen, who were captured on 14 and 17 April respectively, and Seán Lemass, who was later to be responsible for the modernisation of the Irish economy. De Valera was arrested while electioneering in Ennis on 15 August, was kept in solitary confinement for six months and was not released until 16 July 1924. On 14 October 424 prisoners held in Mountjoy went on hunger strike and those held in Kilmainham and other prisons and internment camps joined them. The strike lasted until 23 November, with two hunger strikers dying – Captain Denis Barry on 20 November in Newbridge Camp and Captain Andrew Sullivan in Mountjoy on 22 November.

Most of the internees, not having been convicted of any crime, were freed in the summer of 1924, and a general amnesty was declared on 8 November. One year later the Boundary Commission, which all the Treaty delegates and de Valera believed would allow nationalist areas of Ulster to opt out of the new state of Northern Ireland and help make it ungovernable, proved to be an empty formula. Sir James Craig had declared on 7 October 1925 that if its findings were unacceptable to the Northern Ireland parliament he would resign to lead the defence of any territory 'unfairly transferred'. On 7 November the right-wing *Morning Post* 'leaked' the news that the commission would make no substantial changes, and O'Higgins went to Westminster on the twenty-fourth to prepare the tripartite document that Craig, Stanley Baldwin and Cosgrave would sign on 3 December. The Free State and Northern Ireland were established and the Irish Question seemed finally if unsatisfactorily answered.

The legacy of the Civil War was a chasm in the political and sociological life of the new states; in the South it served as a dire litmus test for all in public life, whether national or local. The first decade of the Free State's existence was menaced by the existence of recently armed and undecommissioned bitter and disappointed men. De Valera's taming and politicising of a majority of these into his newly founded Fianna Fáil party was the greatest of his many services to his country. Cynics marvelled at how it managed to sidestep what a decade before had been the burning question of the oath of allegiance, and its leader proved that for twenty-six counties at least Collins's conviction that the Treaty terms gave the freedom to achieve freedom had been literally true. This was of small comfort to Northern nationalists held in effective thraldom in a discriminatory and one-party state, but their fate had been partially waxed in 1916 by Lloyd George and finally sealed by the death of Michael Collins.

Were they needless deaths after all, those 927 fatalities? They were probably needless but were certainly inevitable given the quasi-religious nature of the struggle and the remarkable personalities of the participants. There is no given reason why the birth pangs of a new state should have been so exquisite or the delivery so bloody. Residual taunters can point to sixteen executions by the British after 1916 and twenty-four during the Anglo-Irish War and compare them with the seventy-seven killed by 'fellow Irishmen'. This kind of insensate rhetoric and the exaltation with which the 'armed struggle' fires its participants is with us still. History *does* teach and those who will not learn its lessons are often forced to endure it again.

BIOGRAPHICAL INDEX

Frank Aiken (1898–1983) was born in Camlough, County Armagh, and became commandant of a division of the IRA in Ulster in 1921. He opposed the Treaty but tried to prevent the outbreak of war. His division engaged in sporadic activity in the mountains near Dundalk and when he became chief of staff of the anti-Treaty forces on the death of *Liam Lynch in April 1923 he used his authority to call off hostilities and issued the order 'to dump arms' on 24 May. He became Minister of Defence in de Valera's first government and held office in each Fianna Fáil administration until 1969. He retired in 1973, having won great respect for Ireland at the United Nations.

Stanley Baldwin (1867–1947) was born in Bewdley, Worcestershire, and educated at Harrow and Trinity College, Cambridge. A steel millionaire, he succeeded *Bonar Law as Conservative leader in 1923 and alternated with Ramsay MacDonald as premier until his resignation in 1937, when he was made Earl Baldwin of Bewdley. He was unfairly blamed for Britain's state of military unreadiness in the face of the Nazi threat but was praised for his handling of the crisis over Edward VIII's abdication. He supported *James Craig in the question of the Boundary Commission's findings in 1925 and was one of the signatories of the agreement which determined the border between Northern Ireland and the Free State.

Harry Boland (1887–1922) was born in Dublin and became secretary of Sinn Féin in 1917. He was one of *Collins's closest friends, was active in the IRB and served as a TD in the first Dáil. He took the anti-Treaty side during the Civil War and was shot while being arrested at Skerries on 31 July 1922.

Dan Breen (1894–1969) was born in Soloheadbeg, County Tipperary, the scene of the ambush in which he and Sean Treacy (1895–1920) were involved on 21 January 1919 and that is regarded as the beginning of the Anglo-Irish War. He continued his guerrilla activity there during the Civil War until his capture on 17 April 1923. The first anti-Treatyite to take his seat in the Dáil in January 1927, he was

Fianna Fáil TD for South Tipperary between 1932 and 1965 and published a distinctly subjective account of his guerrilla activities, *My Fight for Irish Freedom,* in 1924.

Cathal Brugha (1874–1922) was born Charles Burgess in Dublin and founded a firm of candle-makers. He was severely wounded during the fighting in Easter Week, when he was second-in-command to Eamonn Ceannt in the South Dublin Union, but became chief of staff of the IRA in the Anglo-Irish War. He refused to be part of the Treaty delegation and bitterly opposed the settlement. He was shot in Talbot Street in Dublin in the second week of the Civil War.

Erskine Childers (1870–1922) was born in London but reared in County Wicklow. Educated at Haileybury and Cambridge, he fought in the Boer War, became an expert mariner and published the classic adventure story *The Riddle of the Sands* (1903), which postulated a German invasion of England. He became a supporter of Home Rule in 1908 and brought a shipment of arms for the Irish Volunteers on his yacht *Asgard*. He served in the Royal Navy during the Great War, winning the DSC. Although he acted as secretary to the Treaty delegation he became an adamant anti-Treatyite. He was court-martialled for possession of a revolver and executed by firing-squad on 24 November 1922.

Michael Collins (1890–1922) was born in County Cork and served as a civil-service clerk in London. He joined the IRB in 1915 and fought in the GPO during Easter Week. Released from Frongoch in December 1916, he became a significant member of Sinn Féin and the IRA, acting as Minister of Finance from 1919–22. He was a supremely successful head of intelligence during the Anglo-Irish War. He was a reluctant member of the Treaty delegation but saw in its unsatisfactory terms the best that could be obtained at the time and the basis for full independence and the hope of a reunited Ireland. Commander-in-chief of the government forces during the Civil War, he was killed in an ambush in Béal na mBláth, not far from his birthplace, on 22 August 1922.

William Cosgrave (1880–1965) was born in Dublin and was active as a Sinn Féin councillor. He was adjutant to Eamonn Ceannt in the South Dublin Union in Easter Week but a death sentence against him was commuted and he was released under the general amnesty. He replaced *Arthur Griffith as chairman of the Provisional Government in August 1922 and had the responsibility of carrying on the Civil War, which he did with great distress and an equally stern sense of duty. His was the sure if conservative hand that shaped and stabilised the new Free State; during his years of office he had to face continuing republican activity, a mutiny in the army and the loss of his brilliant and enigmatic Minister for Justice, *Kevin O'Higgins. He was one of the founders of Fine Gael (1933) and its leader from 1935 until his retirement in 1944.

James Craig (1971–1940) was born in Belfast and educated in Edinburgh. He was Edward Carson's lieutenant during the anti-Home Rule agitation in 1913 and leader of the Ulster Unionists at the founding of the Northern Ireland state in 1921, becoming its first prime minister. He made sure of local and provincial unionist political domination by the abolition of proportional representation in 1929 and effectively neutered the Boundary Commission by threats, non-cooperation and the fact that he was confident of support from *Stanley Baldwin, the British prime minister. Though instinctively less sectarian that some of his cabinet colleagues, he made no effort to curb their anti-Catholic legislation. Knighted in 1918, he was created Viscount Craigavon in 1927.

Liam Deasy (1898–1974) was born near Bandon, County Cork, and was adjutant of the west Cork brigade of the IRA during the Anglo-Irish War. He rejected the Treaty and though he fought in the Civil War was greatly distressed by its effects. He believed that the surrender of the Four Courts should have meant the end rather than the beginning of hostilities. He was captured by government forces in January 1923 and, convinced that the time had come to end the fighting, signed an instrument worded for him by his captors that he was in favour of unconditional surrender. After the war he took

no further part in public life but served throughout the Emergency in the Irish army. He
published a book on the Civil War called *Brother
against Brother*.

Éamon de Valera (1882–1975) was born in New
York but was brought up in County Limerick from
the age of two. He became a lecturer in mathematics
and joined the Gaelic League in 1908 and the
Volunteers in 1914. Commander at Boland's Mills
during Easter Week, he was the only 1916 leader
to survive a sentence of execution, largely due to
the efforts of John Redmond (1856–1918) and
John Dillon (1851–1927). He was president of the
first Dáil Éireann and the first leader to meet
*Lloyd George after the truce which ended the
Anglo-Irish War in 1921. He refused to lead the
Treaty delegation and rejected the terms agreed by
*Collins and *Griffith. Largely inactive during the
Civil War, he signed the order of cessation of
hostilities in 1923. His greatest postwar achieve-
ment was the politicisation of the republican
movement by the founding of the Fianna Fáil
party, which he led as Taoiseach in four governments. He also served two terms as president
(1959–73).

Arthur Griffith (1871–1922) was born in Dublin and became a journalist, a member of the Gaelic League and the IRB and the founder in 1906 of Sinn Féin, an organisation which urged Irish self-sufficiency and passive resistance as the means of ending British rule. He opposed the Home Rule bill of 1914 and, although not a participant, was arrested after the Easter Rising. As leader of the Treaty delegation he was first signatory of the agreement. Elected president of the second Dáil after the resignation of *de Valera, he died of a cerebral haemorrhage on 12 August 1922.

Andrew Bonar Law (1858–1923) was born in Canada but worked as an iron merchant in Glasgow, serving as a Unionist MP from 1910. He replaced Arthur Balfour (1848–1930) as Unionist leader in the House of Commons. He actively supported Ulster's resistance to Home Rule and left *Lloyd George with little room to manoeuvre during the Treaty negotiations. He replaced him as prime minister (1922–3).

Seán Lemass (1899–1971) was born in Ballybrack, County Dublin, and as a fifteen-year-old fought in the GPO in 1916. He opposed the

Treaty and was active in the Wicklow Mountains after the surrender of the Four Courts. Interned in 1923, he decided that the republican ideal must be attained by political means rather than by force of arms. He was one of the architects of the Fianna Fáil party and was foremost in developing Ireland's potential as a modern European nation. He served as Taoiseach from 1959–66 and in 1965 made the significant offer of friendship to Terence O'Neill, then Stormont prime minister.

David Lloyd George (1863–1945) was born in Manchester but brought up near Criccieth in Wales. He had a brilliant career as an advanced Liberal statesman, associated with such important early welfare legislation as the Old Age Pensions Act (1908) and the National Insurance Act (1911), and with the Parliament Act (1911), which tamed the House of Lords. Always a supporter of special treatment for Ulster unionists, probably because of his Welsh-chapel upbringing, he determined on exclusion for them as early as 1916, a decision which pleased neither Edward Carson (1854–1935) nor John Redmond (1856–

1918). He led the British delegation at the Treaty talks, insisted on the oath of allegiance to the monarch and threatened 'war within three days' if his terms were not accepted. He hoped that the Ulster exclusion would be temporary and was hampered during the period by the need to placate *Bonar Law's Conservatives. In spite of this he was forced to resign in 1922 and never held office again. His political eclipse meant the effective end of the Liberal party.

Liam Lynch (1893-1923) was born in County Limerick and worked in a hardware business until 1919, when he organised the Cork Volunteers. He then became an able brigade commander during the Anglo-Irish War. He opposed the Treaty and was anxious to avoid a conflict but after the beginning of the Civil War became the most implacable of commanders. He led the Southern division of the Irregulars and hoped to hold a 'Munster Republic' against the Free State forces. He was mortally wounded in the Knockmealdown mountains in County Waterford on 10 April 1923.

Seán Mac Eoin (1894–1973), known as the 'Blacksmith of Ballinalee' (in County Longford), led a flying column there during the Anglo-Irish War. He supported the Treaty and became chief of staff of the Free State army. He resigned in 1929 to become a TD and served as Fine Gael minister in both the inter-party governments. He stood unsuccessfully for the presidency in 1945 and 1959.

Eoin MacNeill (1867–1945) was born in Glenarm, County Antrim, and became a self-taught Gaelic scholar, serving as professor of Early and Medieval Irish History in UCD between 1909 and 1941. He was a founder of the Irish Volunteers in 1913 but countermanded the order for the Easter Rising in 1916. He was Minister for Finance in the First Dáil and Minister for Education in the Executive Council of the Free State. A member of the Boundary Commission (1924–5), which was to review the partition of Ireland, he resigned, refusing to accept its findings. He was president of the Royal Irish Academy between 1940 and 1943.

Liam Mellows (1892–1922) was born in Manchester but reared in County Wexford. He was a member of Fianna Éireann (the youth organisation of the Volunteers), was strongly influenced by the views of James Connolly (1868–1916) and fought in minor actions in Galway during Easter Week. He escaped to America, where he worked with John Devoy (1842–1928) on the *Gaelic American* and organised *de Valera's eighteen-month fund-raising tour of America (1919-20). IRA director of purchases, he considered the Treaty a betrayal of the republic and wished to establish a revolutionary counter to the Provisional Government. He was part of the Four Courts garrison and, like his comrade *Rory O'Connor, was executed in Mountjoy on 8 December 1922, the day after the assassination of Sean Hales TD, a member of the government, as a deterrent against further killings of public representatives.

Richard Mulcahy (1886–1971) was born in Waterford and worked as a post-office clerk. He was involved in the ambush at Ashbourne during Easter Week and after the general amnesty became a senior figure in the IRA. He supported the Treaty and as commander-in-chief after *Collins's death was vigorous in his activity against the Irregulars. He was one of the founders of the Fine Gael party in 1933 and, precluded because of his Civil War reputation from the post of Taoiseach in the coalition governments of the 1940s and 1950s, served as Minister of Education under John A. Costello (1891–1976).

Rory O'Connor (1883–1922) was born in Dublin and worked as a railway engineer in Canada. Interned after the Easter Rising, he was director of engineering during the Anglo-Irish War and became a leader of the Irregulars, the members of the IRA who were determined to fight against the agreement. He set up the republican garrison in the Four Courts in April 1922 and was arrested at its surrender in June. He was executed on 8 December in Mountjoy with three other republicans – *Liam Mellows, Richard Barrett and Joseph McKelvey – as a reprisal for the killing, the previous day, of Sean Hales TD, a member of the Provisional Government, and as a deterrent against similar assassinations of public representatives.

Eoin O'Duffy (1892–1944) was born near Castleblayney, County Monaghan, and trained as an engineer. He fought in the Anglo-Irish War, becoming chief of staff of the IRA in succession to *Richard Mulcahy. He supported the Treaty and became commissioner of the Garda Síochána. He was dismissed from the post in 1933 when *de Valera became Taoiseach and in July that year formed the Army Comrades' Association. The name of the group was changed to the National Guard and it was intended as a protective force for the Fine Gael party against the attacks of Fianna Fáil supporters. With their fascist trappings and distinctive uniforms, the members became known as the 'Blueshirts'. *William Cosgrave disapproved of the National Guard's undemocratic aura and the movement gradually disintegrated. In 1936 O'Duffy organised an Irish Brigade to fight for Franco in the Spanish Civil War, in spite of Ireland's official policy of non-interference. When he died on 30 November 1944 he was given a state funeral.

Kevin O'Higgins (1892–1927) was born in Stradbally, Queen's County, and educated at Clongowes, Maynooth and UCD. He joined Sinn Féin and was imprisoned for making an anti-conscription speech in 1918. He was a strong Treatyite and the architect of the Garda Síochána, the acceptable civilian police force, and he took vigorous measures to restore law and order to a war-torn country. He drew up the list of special powers arrogated by the army in October 1922 and was one of the signatories of the order to execute Rory O'Connor (who had been his best man), Liam Mellows and two others in exemplary reprisal for the shooting of Sean Hales TD. This was the probable cause of the shooting of his father in February 1923 and of his own killing by republicans in July 1927.

Ernie O'Malley (1898–1957) was born in Castlebar and was a medical student in UCD when he fought in Easter Week. He was active during the Anglo-Irish War and, opposing the Treaty, was appointed a member of the IRA Army Council in October 1922. He was badly wounded and captured by government forces in November 1922; after recovering from his wounds he went on a hunger strike which lasted for forty-one days in Mountjoy. His death sentence was commuted when the surgeons said he would never walk again. He was elected abstentionist TD for North Dublin in 1923 and released in July 1924. Having recovered the use of his limbs he travelled widely and was one of the chief fund-raisers for the *Irish Press*. His accounts of his experiences in the Anglo-Irish War – *On Another Man's Wound* (1936) – and the Civil War – *The Singing Flame* (1978) – are regarded as the finest literary record of the events of the two conflicts.

Austin Stack (1879-1929) was born near Tralee, County Kerry, and was arrested for his involvement in the attempted landing of arms by Sir Roger Casement (1864–1916) at Banna Strand in April 1916. He was Minister for Home Affairs in the first Dáil and a member of the Treaty delegation. He rejected the terms of the Treaty and was active in the Civil War until his capture in April 1923. During his imprisonment in Kilmainham he led a hunger strike for forty-one days, an ordeal from which his health never recovered.

Oscar Traynor (1886–1963) was born in Dublin and trained as a wood-carver and compositor. He took part in the 1916 Rising and was interned at Frongoch. Commander of the Dublin brigade of the IRA, he led the attack on the Customs House on 25 May 1921. He opposed the Treaty and continued to organise military activity in Wicklow after the battle for Dublin. He served in most Fianna Fáil governments until his resignation because of ill-health in 1961. A noted footballer, he played for Belfast Celtic when he was a young man and was president of the FAI from 1948 until his death.

SELECT BIBLIOGRAPHY

Connolly, S (ed.). *The Oxford Companion to Irish History*. Oxford, 1998.

Coogan, T. P. *Michael Collins*. London, 1990.

Deasy, L. *Brother against Brother*. Cork, 1998.

Doherty, J. E. and Hickey, D. J. *A Chronology of Irish History since 1500*. Dublin, 1989.

Dwyer, T. Ryle. *De Valera*. Dublin, 1991.

Fanning, R. *Independent Ireland*. Dublin, 1983.

Foster, R. F. *Modern Ireland 1600–1972*. London, 1988.

Griffith, K. and T. O'Grady (eds.). *Curious Journey*. Cork, 1998.

Kee, R. The Green Flag. London, 1970.

Lee, J. J. *Ireland 1912–1985*. Cambridge, 1989.

Lyons, F. S. L. *Ireland since the Famine*. London, 1971.

Macardle, D. *The Irish Republic*. Dublin, 1937 (revised 1968).

Neeson, E. *The Civil War 1922–23*. Dublin, 1989.

Ó Gadhra, N. *Civil War in Connacht 1922–1923*. Cork, 1999.

O'Malley, E. *The Singing Flame*. Dublin, 1978.